Design a garden for me on pages 34-35.

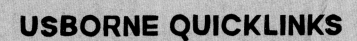

USBORNE QUICKLINKS

Scan the code for links to websites where you can find even more ideas for things to make and do, or go to **usborne.com/Quicklinks** and type in the title of this book.

Please follow the internet safety guidelines at Usborne Quicklinks. Children should be supervised online.

CARDBOARD BOX BASICS

Here are some tips and tricks for you to use when you're doing all the things in this book.

TYPES OF BOXES

The cardboard used to make boxes comes in different thicknesses...

THIN cardboard is easier to bend.

Corrugated cardboard is **THICK**. It's made up of layers – with a wavy layer in the middle.

Felt-tip pens don't work well on boxes that have a shiny surface.

You can write on the other side that's rough.

FLAPS

At the top and bottom of most types of boxes, you'll find flaps.

They can have four flaps...

...or two small flaps and a big flap that tucks over them.

You can unfold these boxes so they're **FLAT**...

1 Open out all the flaps.

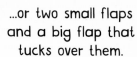

2 Press the box flat and cut along one of the joins to open it out.

This works for boxes of all sizes.

TRACING

On some pages, you'll find pictures to trace. If you don't have any tracing paper, you can use baking parchment paper or very thin white paper instead.

4

USBORNE ACTIVITIES

WHAT CAN I DO WITH A...
CARDBOARD BOX?

James Maclaine

Illustrated by
Harriet Noble and Erin Wallace

Designed by
Jenny Offley, Jodie Smith
and Helen Cooke

CONTENTS

I wonder which project you'll do first...

Turn to pages 10-11 to make a model dinosaur.

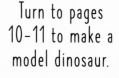

CRAYONS AND PAINT

See what happens when you hold a crayon on its side and rub it firmly over corrugated cardboard.

The ridges inside the cardboard should make a textured rubbing.

When painting boxes, you might need to wait for the paint to dry before adding another layer...

...unless you want the original design to show through. This can look interesting!

TUBES

To cut the end off a cardboard tube neatly...

1 Wrap a piece of tape around the tube.

2 Cut into the tube. Stop when you reach the far side of the tape.

3 Then cut around the tube, along the edge of the tape.

CARDBOARD SCRAPS

And remember to **RECYCLE** any leftover pieces of cardboard – or **REUSE** them if you can...

Strips for bookmarks

Rectangles of cardboard with a shiny surface are useful as glue spreaders.

The lid from an egg carton can be used as a paint tray.

Somewhere to make notes or sketches

TISSUE BOX
MONSTERS

Looking at an empty box of tissues, you might see nothing more than a box with a hole in it. But that hole can easily become...

...A MONSTER'S GAPING MOUTH.

If there's any plastic inside the hole, cut it away first.

Now you just need to cut out paper shapes for different body parts and stick them on.

You could add some **SPOTS**.

Use yellow paper if your monster hasn't brushed its teeth in a while.

TEETH

Rectangles for peg-shaped teeth

Long triangles for fangs

Glue the teeth around the hole, inside the box.

EYES

Egg shapes and circles

Stick them together in size order.

HORNS

Fold the ends of horn shapes, to make short tabs. Then attach the tabs to the box, so the horns stick up.

Stick thin strips over its body for **STRIPES**.

Wide tissue boxes are perfect for making **BIG MONSTERS**.

TAKE AIM...

Here's a game you can play with your monster.

1 Scrunch up little pieces of waste paper into balls...

2 ...and try to throw them into its mouth.

3 Stand further and further away. What happens to your aim?

BOX MUSEUM

If you turn a big box into a building for your own museum, you can fill it with any collection of things you like.

1 Stand a box on its smallest side.

Open out the flaps.

Cut off this flap at the bottom.

2 Draw a line for a roof shape on this flap. Then cut along it.

The roof should stay up.

Cut off the bottom corners to make an entrance into your museum.

3 Draw and cut out signs and windows to stick inside the box.

4 Now display things you've collected or made...

DISPLAY IDEAS

Stand items on top of the smallest boxes you can find.

Look out for cardboard containers of unusual shapes, to use as plinths.

To make a mini cabinet, take a small box and cut off the flaps.

TICK

SLOT TOGETHER STEGOSAURUS

The templates on these pages will help you to make a cardboard Stegosaurus that's sturdy enough to stand up.

1  Put some tracing paper over each template. Then use a pencil to draw over all the black lines that show through.

2 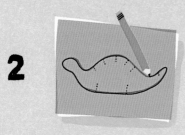 Turn over the paper and place it on top of some flat cardboard. Draw over all the lines, pressing hard.

3  The pencil lines should show on the cardboard. Now cut out all the shapes you traced.

4  Cut slits into the pieces following all the dotted lines.

5 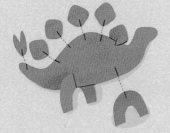 Then slot the legs onto the body, the plates along the back and the spikes at the end of the tail.

TEMPLATES

LEGS

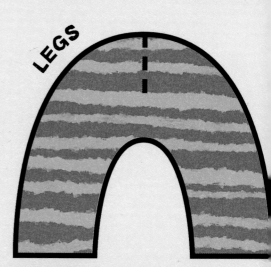

 To make some cardboard leaves for your Stegosaurus, cut slits into shapes like these.

10

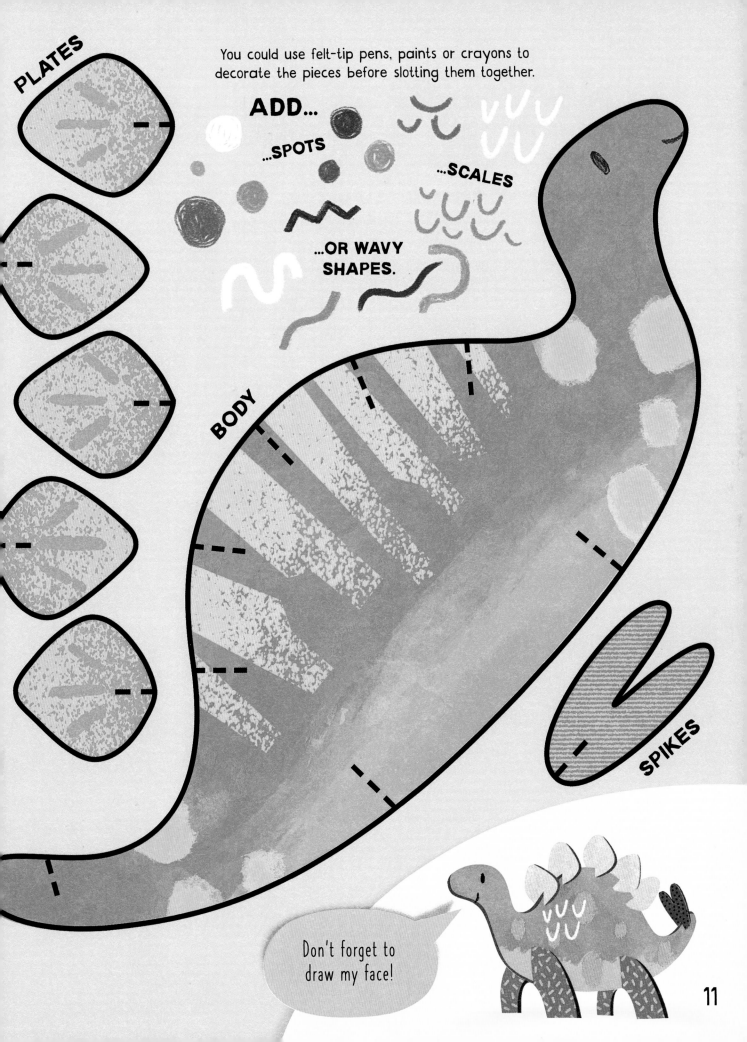

TOUCAN CALENDAR

Next time you start a new tube of toothpaste, save the long, narrow box to make this calendar. It's reusable year after year – and there's a compartment for you to keep your pens and pencils tidy.

TUESDAY

OCTOBER

25

You could also write your name on the front.

Mia

FIRST, TURN THE BOX INTO TWO BOXES.

1 Open the flaps at both ends of your toothpaste box. Then flatten the box.

2 Use a ruler to draw a line 4cm (1.5in) above the flaps at one end. Cut across the box, following the line.

4cm

1.5in

Use this piece in the next step.

Save this piece for step 5.

3 Glue the flaps back together and turn the box upside down.

Copy these three black lines onto it.

4 Turn over the box and cut along all the lines you drew in step 3.

5 Take the piece left over from step 2. Draw a line 8cm (3in) below the flaps. Cut along the line and glue the flaps back together to make the second box.

8cm

3in

Keep this piece for step 7.

6 Use more glue to stick both the boxes you've made together, side by side.

7 Take the piece left over from step 5. Cut along one corner.

Press the cardboard flat and cut off one of the sides.

Use this strip in step 8.

Save this piece for step 9.

8 Glue the boxes on top of the cardboard strip, in the middle.

9 Draw a toucan on the back of the piece you saved, like this.

Cut it out and glue it to the front of the tall box.

TURN THE PAGE...

Now make cards to show the date, month and day.

1 Use a ruler to mark dots every 4cm (1.5in) across a big piece of thick paper, in three rows, like this.

2 Connect the dots with straight lines down the paper.

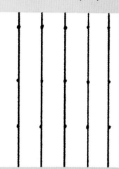

3 Next, draw straight lines across the paper, 8cm (3in) above the bottom, then 6.5cm (2.5in) higher up and then every 5cm (2in) until you reach the top.

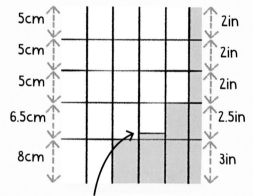

5cm — 2in
5cm — 2in
5cm — 2in
6.5cm — 2.5in
8cm — 3in

Add a line here to make one more rectangle that's 5cm (2in) high.

4 Cut along the lines to make 16 short rectangles, three medium rectangles and two tall rectangles.

5 Use a black pen to write a big **1** on the front of the first **SHORT** rectangle. Then write a big **2** on the back. Add the numbers **3** to **31** to the rest of the short rectangles.

1 **2** **3**

6 Write **JANUARY** at the top of the first **MEDIUM** rectangle. Then rotate it and write **FEBRUARY** at the top.

JANUARY   MARCH

FEBRUARY   APRIL

Turn it over to add **MARCH** and **APRIL** on the back. Use the other two medium rectangles for the next eight months.

7 On the front of the first **TALL** rectangle, write **MONDAY** and **TUESDAY**, like this.

MONDAY   WEDNESDAY

TUESDAY   THURSDAY

Then write **WEDNESDAY** and **THURSDAY** on the back. Write the rest of the days of the week on the second tall rectangle.

8 Stand all the cards in order, in the short box. Rotate the cards and move them to the back of each set as the date changes.

SUNDAY
JUNE
26

MARBLE MAZE

Copy the layout of this big box lid, gluing down different cardboard items to create obstacles in a maze. Holding it **FLAT** between your hands, tilt the lid to guide the marble all the way to the goal as quickly as you can.

Draw a spot for the start and arrows to show the route.

ZIGZAG TRACK

Draw a zigzag across a rectangle of thick cardboard. Cut along the line.

Then glue down the two pieces so they're slightly more than a marble's width apart.

BUMPERS

Stick on cardboard circles and triangles to block off parts of your maze.

TUNNELS

Cut cardboard tubes into tunnels of different lengths.

What else could you use instead of marbles? Test beads, balls of scrunched-up foil and any other round things.

GOAL

1 Cut off the top of a small box. Turn it upside down. Draw an arch shape that's wider than your marble on the front.

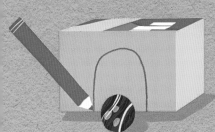

2 Cut along the line. Then make little cuts – about 1.5cm (0.5in) long – into the four corners of the box.

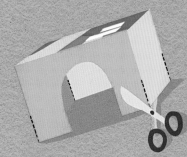

3 Fold them back to make little tabs. Glue the tabs to the inside of the lid to attach the goal.

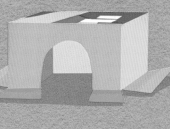

CHUNKY BEADS

You might not expect to wear a necklace made from a box of corn flakes... **BUT** because they're usually decorated with eye-catching designs, cereal boxes and other types of food packaging are the ideal source of cardboard for rolling into bright beads.

1 Cut the cardboard into long, thin strips.

2 Mark the top of each strip, in the middle, and then draw two diagonal lines to the sides.

Cut along the lines.

3 Press down firmly on the back of each strip with a thin paintbrush, near the tip.

Then pull the strip through. Do it again. (This makes the cardboard easier to roll.)

4 Dab glue over the back of each strip, leaving the bottom part unglued at the wide end.

5 Roll the unglued end **TIGHTLY** around the brush. Keep rolling all the way to the tip, to make your bead.

6 Now slide off the bead and leave it to dry.

If the tip is loose, use more glue to stick it down – or snip it off.

TUBES

To make tube-shaped beads, like these, simply skip step 2.

BRACELET

Thread lots of beads onto some string or thin ribbon. Then tie a knot to join the ends together.

BOX SEAT

Even big cardboard boxes aren't usually sturdy enough for you to sit on – unless you know a couple of tricks for making them **STRONGER**...

TRICK 1: SPIRAL SUPPORTS

1 Place the box on its longest side on a big, flat piece of cardboard. Draw around it.

2 Repeat step 1, then cut out both rectangles.

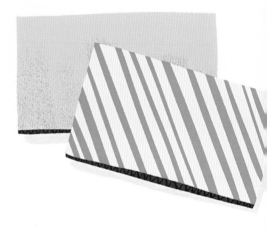

3 Roll up each rectangle from its shortest end into a spiral.

4 Open up all four flaps at the top and stand the spirals inside the box.

5 Close the two longest flaps and join them together with a long piece of masking tape

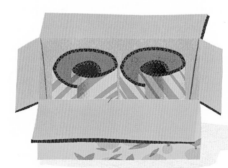

NOW SIT ON THE BOX...

Can the box support you even if you lift your feet off the floor?

Next, add more cardboard spirals inside...

Do they make the box feel sturdier?

TRICK 2: STRONG FOLDS

1 First, peel off any old pieces of tape from another big box. Then open all the flaps at the top and bottom.

2 Turn the box upside down. Fold in all four flaps, so they touch the insides.

3 Turn over the box. Fold in both the long flaps, but leave the two short flaps pointing up.

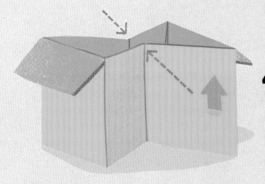

4 Hold both long edges at the top, halfway across. Push them together, so the sides bend in.

5 Now fold down the two short flaps, so they meet in the middle. Stick long pieces of masking tape along and across the join, to secure the flaps together.

...AND SIT ON THIS BOX TOO.

Which trick turns the box into the strongest stool?

Can you think of any other ways to strengthen boxes?

JIGSAW PUZZLE

Turn a picture that you've drawn, printed out or found in an old magazine into a jigsaw puzzle...

1 Choose a picture with lots of details.

2 Spread glue all over the back. Stick it onto some cardboard and then cut around the edges.

3 Place a pile of heavy books on top. This stops the cardboard from curling as it dries.

4 Draw a pattern of simple shapes on the back, like these.

5 Cut out all the pieces and shuffle them so they're jumbled up.

Now how quickly can you put your picture back together?

20

FABULOUS FRAME

Here's an idea for a shiny frame to show off one of your pictures. Reuse a clean piece of foil as well as cardboard, glue and string to make it.

1 Cut out two squares or rectangles of cardboard the size you want your frame to be.

Place your picture in the middle of one piece and draw around it.

2 Remove the picture. Draw a straight line from each corner to the nearest corner of the cardboard, like this.

Then cut along all the lines. You don't need to keep the middle.

3 Stick the frame pieces from step 2 on top of the other piece of cardboard.

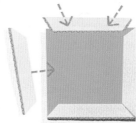

4 Then glue pieces of string onto the frame, to make wiggly patterns.

5 Spread glue on the back of a big piece of foil, then place it over the whole frame.

Carefully wrap the edges of the foil behind the frame.

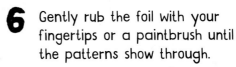

6 Gently rub the foil with your fingertips or a paintbrush until the patterns show through.

And stick your picture in the middle.

KEEPING COMICS SAFE

You can reshape cereal boxes and cover them with old wrapping paper for storing any comic books you collect, pictures you draw or stories you write.

RESHAPE THE BOX...

1 Carefully cut off the flaps at the top of a cereal box.

2 Mark the middle of the left-hand edge with a dot. Then draw a straight line between the dot and the top right corner.

3 Cut along the line and down the edge to the dot. Keep this triangle for the next step.

4 Turn over the triangle and place it on the other side of the box. Draw a line along the edge.

5 Cut along the line and then straight across the side of the box.

FORTIS
SOUVENIR ISSUE
PART 2

POT

1 Turn over a big piece of used wrapping paper. Stick the base of the box in the middle with lots of glue. Wait for it to dry.

2 Tip the box onto the smallest of its sides. Then draw around the edges on the paper.

3 Tip the box onto its other three sides and draw around them too.

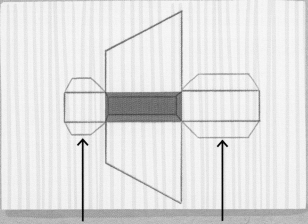

4 Use a ruler to draw four tabs (shown in blue) next to these sides. Then cut around the outside edge of the tabs and the other shapes.

5 Glue the paper to the box, wrapping the tabs around the front and back first. Then fold up the rest of the paper and stick it on.

JEN'S DOODLES

KEEP OUT

NOW STICK ON LABELS...

Cut out shapes from plain paper or pictures from magazines to customize your boxes.

SUPERHEROES

ANIMAL ART

My POEMS

23

MINI VILLAGE

Here are some ideas for cardboard box buildings.
You'll find the instructions for how to make the roofs, doors
and windows at the bottom of the next four pages.

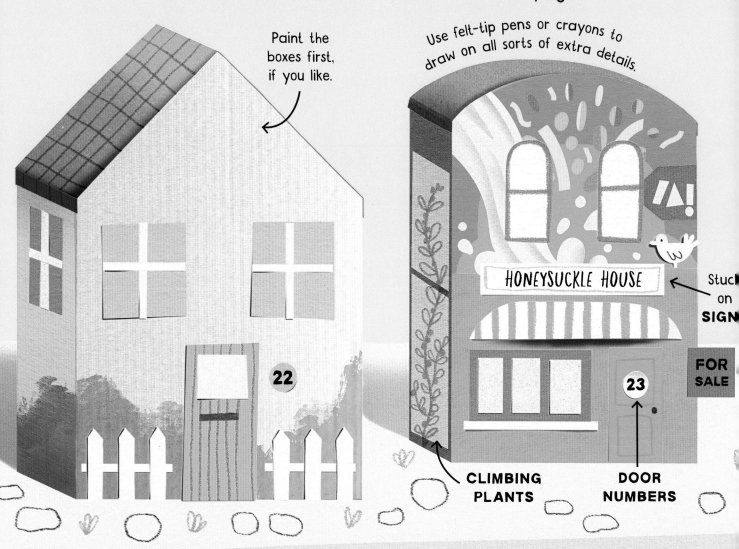

Paint the
boxes first,
if you like.

Use felt-tip pens or crayons to
draw on all sorts of extra details.

HONEYSUCKLE HOUSE

Stuc
on
SIGN

FOR
SALE

22

23

**CLIMBING
PLANTS**

**DOOR
NUMBERS**

ROOFS

Cut off any flaps at the top of each box, then follow
these red lines to cut it into the shape you want...

PITCHED

CURVED

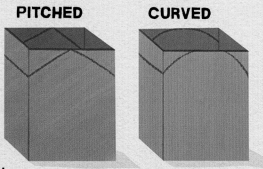

To give it a roof,
fold or curve a
wide strip of thick
paper around the
opening and stick
the ends to the
sides of the box.

To make a **CONE-SHAPED** roof...

Draw around
a mug or
bowl on a
piece of paper.

Cut out the circle.
Then cut into the middle.

Stick this
side onto
here.

Now stick it to the
top of a box.

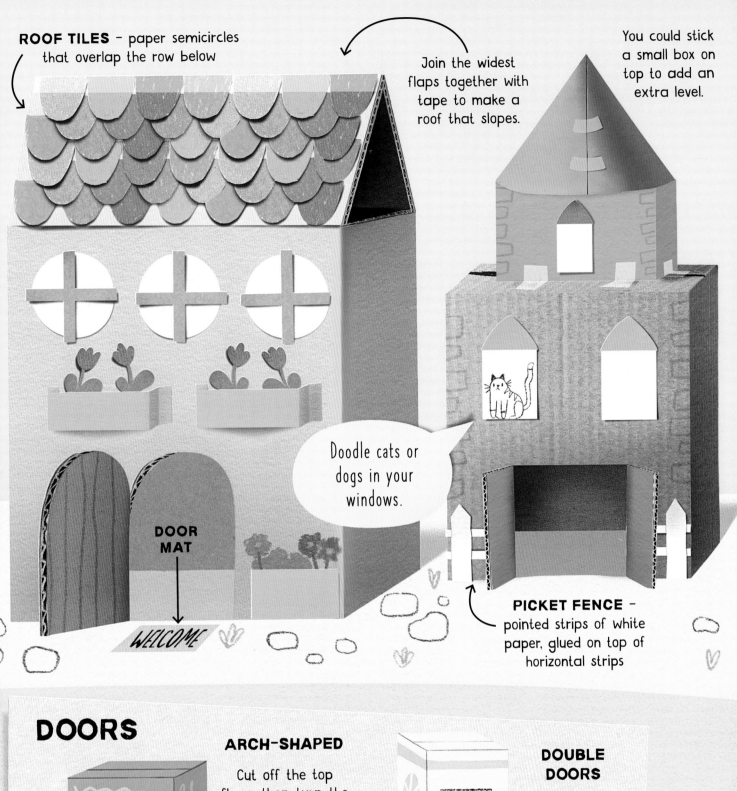

ROOF TILES – paper semicircles that overlap the row below

Join the widest flaps together with tape to make a roof that slopes.

You could stick a small box on top to add an extra level.

Doodle cats or dogs in your windows.

DOOR MAT

WELCOME

PICKET FENCE – pointed strips of white paper, glued on top of horizontal strips

DOORS

ARCH-SHAPED

Cut off the top flaps, then turn the box upside down.

Draw this line on the front.

Cut along the line and fold back the door.

DOUBLE DOORS

Draw a big T to cut along instead.

Then fold back both sides to open out the doors.

TURN THE PAGE...

Four-sided **ROOF TILES**

LIBRARY

12
9 · · 3
6

CLOCK FACE –
numbers and hands
drawn on in pen

BAKERY

TODAY
SOURDOUGH
BREAD
CROISSANTS
CAKES

SHOP SIGN –
made from a strip
of cardboard
folded in half

BRICKS - printed onto the box by dipping the end of
a rectangular eraser into red paint and pressing it on

WINDOWS
Copy one of these window
shapes onto paper. Cut it out,
then add a pair of shutters.

Draw around
the window
on a different
piece of paper.

Add a line down
the middle...

...and rectangles
for tabs.

Stick the
window onto
the box.

Then cut out each
shutter and stick its
tab to the left or
right of the window.

Tape a cardboard tube to the side of a box for a **ROUND TOWER**. Then stick a cone-shaped roof on top.

Cut out squares from the top edges to make **RAMPARTS**, like these.

Glue very thin strips of paper inside the box, so they hang over a door.

28

STEPS

Cut out three rectangles of different widths, using corrugated cardboard.

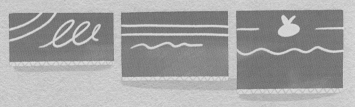

Stick them on top of each other, in size order.

BALCONIES AND WINDOW BOXES

Draw three squares or rectangles side by side on thin cardboard.

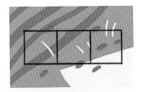

Add a narrow rectangle at each end for tabs.

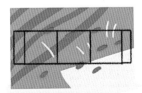

Cut around the outer edge.

Then fold along all the lines and glue the tabs onto the box.

CRISSCROSS PATTERNS

See what patterns you can create by making lots of little holes in cardboard shapes and then threading pieces of string or yarn through them.

1 Cut out a rectangle, square, triangle or semicircle – or any shape you like – from cardboard. The bigger, the better!

2 Push the tip of a pencil into the shape, to make an even number of holes. Do this on top of a thick piece of cardboard to protect the table underneath.

3 Then use the pencil to push the ends of a long piece of string or yarn through any pair of holes.

4 On the other side of the cardboard, pull both ends tight and tie a knot.

5 Repeat steps 3 and 4 until you've connected every pair of holes.

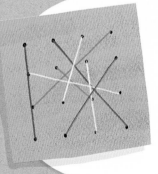
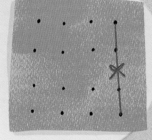

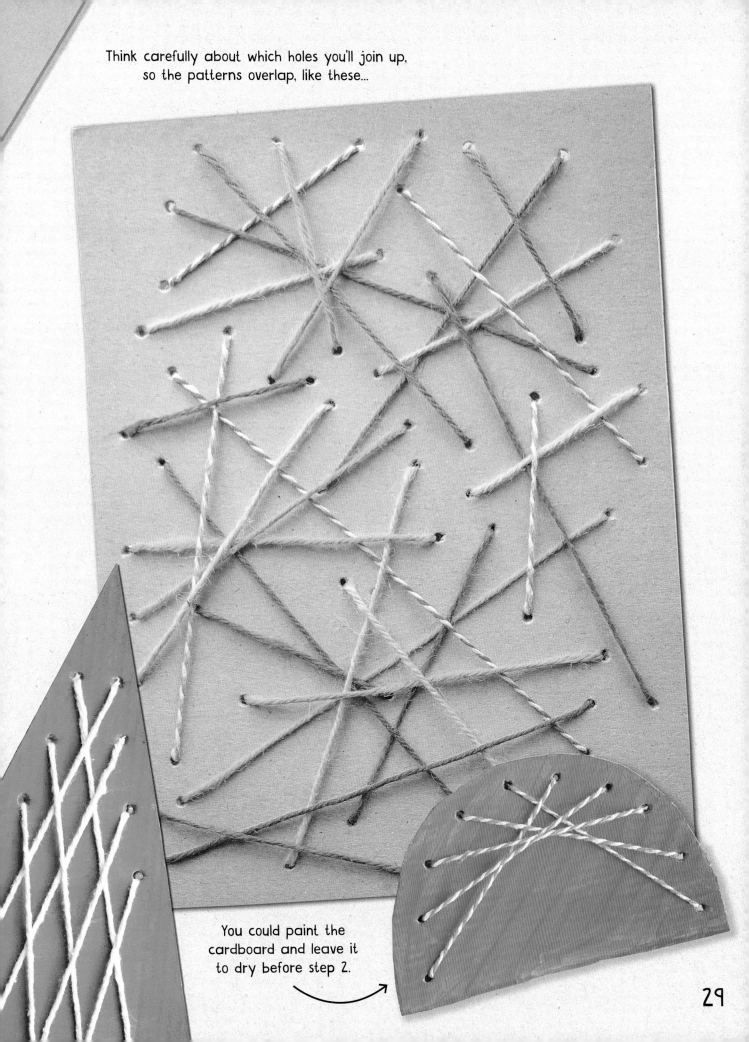

Think carefully about which holes you'll join up,
so the patterns overlap, like these...

You could paint the
cardboard and leave it
to dry before step 2.

SUPER TARGETS

Turn big boxes, paper cups, string and cardboard tubes into an exciting array of targets for you to perfect your aim. If you're playing with a friend, decide where you have to stand or kneel before you take a shot.

DROP SHOT

1 Cut off all the flaps at the bottom of the box. Then draw a circle on the top, **ACROSS** the two biggest flaps.

2 Cut out the half circle from each flap.

3 Tape the flaps together on either side of the hole.

Now toss small balls in here.

ARCHES

Cut out arches of different shapes and sizes.

Flick as many coins as you can through each one.

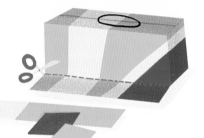

Stick long strips of masking tape onto the floor to show where the coins have to stay inside.

After you've scored, lift up the box to collect the balls or coins.

BALANCING BALLS

Use lots of tape to stick cardboard tubes of different heights on top of a box.

Balance a lightweight ball on top. Then throw another ball to knock it off.

If you don't have any balls, scrunch up paper to play with instead.

Write numbers on your targets to show how many points each one scores.

9 **5**

HANGING CUP

Follow the steps on the right to create a hanging cup. Then guide the string into a slit you've snipped into the top of your box.

If your ball hits the target, the cup will swing.

1 Make a hole in the base of a paper cup with the tip of a pencil.

2 Thread through a piece of string and tie a big knot at each end.

3 Stick on paper circles to decorate the cup before you hang it.

ENGINEERING WITH CARDBOARD

Engineers build models to test out solutions to different problems. You can do the same using leftover pieces of cardboard.

MAKE A BETTER BRIDGE

1 Balance a long, wide strip of thin cardboard between two stacks of books, the same height as each other.

2 Stand different tubs and boxes on top. The heavier they are, the more the bridge will **BEND**.

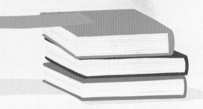

3 Now make a fold as wide as your thumb from the long edge of the strip.

4 Turn it over to fold the first fold back on itself.

5 Keep turning and folding the strip all the way across. Can it support heavy tubs now?

HOW IT WORKS

The folds spread out the force of the tub pushing down, so the bridge can support more weight.

RAMP IT UP

Investigate how ramps help to move things smoothly up or down uneven surfaces.

First, tie a long piece of string to a heavy pencil case.

Then lift the case over a chair by tugging the string between your fingers.

Now use a big piece of cardboard for a ramp or tape two pieces together. Lean it on the chair. Does it feel easier to pull the pencil case up the ramp?

Next, watch how quickly a roll of tape moves down the ramp. Stand the tape on its edge at the top and let go...

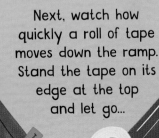

ZOOOOM

THE SECRET OF THE
ROMAN ARCH

Ancient Roman engineers knew that the blocks in a rounded arch stay up by pressing against each other. Follow these steps to see how...

1 Put a piece of tracing paper on top of the template on the right. Then use a ruler and pencil to trace all the black lines. Turn over the paper. Put it on top of some thin corrugated cardboard and draw over the lines.

2 Cut out the big rectangle. Draw along the dividing lines, pressing firmly. This makes the cardboard much easier to fold.

3 Fold along the lines and glue the short ends together, to make a wedge shape. Then make six more...

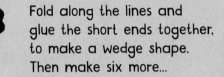  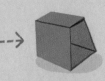 **x7**

4 Ask someone to help you to arrange the pieces as shown in the picture below. You won't need any more glue, but you'll need to stack some coins in the bottom two wedges, to weigh them down.

> Even arches made of stone stay up without any cement.

The piece in the middle is called the keystone. It has such an important-sounding name because your arch will tumble if you dare to pull it out.

INDOOR GARDEN IN A BOX

Use the ideas on these pages and your own imagination to design a garden that can fit inside a big, shallow box.

1 If your box has any flaps, cut them off first.

2 Then half-fill the box with sand, gravel or dry compost if you have it.

3 Now push things in or place them on top to make your garden...

Write down and sketch out your ideas to help you to plan your design.

Nature pond

Hanging decoration
Could reuse junk mail

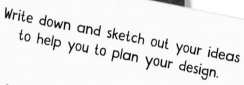

Wild garden?

Somewhere to sit

Shed
Paint blue?

PATIO

Cut up scraps of cardboard into little squares or rectangles.

PLANTS

Cut out shapes like these from thin cardboard. Stick them to the inside edge of the box for bushes.

Draw lines on the sides of the box, to make them look like brick walls.

HANGING DECORATION

Push in two pencils and tie some thread between them.

Then cut out little triangles from junk mail and glue them, back to back, on either side of the thread.

WATER FEATURE

Save small foil trays to fill with water for a pond or swimming pool.

Cover parts of the compost with pencil shavings to look like bark. Then pile up cardboard strips for logs where insects can hide.

Add some pebbles for a rock garden or stepping stones.

SHED

1 First, open up the flaps at the top of a little box and cut them off.

Following the red lines, cut down and across one side only.

Fold back the cardboard to make a door.

2 Now turn the box over.

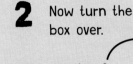

Fold a strip of paper in half for a roof. Glue the edges to opposite sides of the box.

Then stick on shapes for door hinges and a window.

THE AMAZING PAINTING MACHINE

With the lid of a shoebox, a few marbles and some paints,
you can make all sorts of surprising pictures.

1 Using masking tape, stick a piece of paper inside the shoebox lid. Then place a marble on top.

2 Next, drip a little paint onto the paper.

3 Holding the lid between both hands, tilt it up, down and from side to side. Watch the marble roll through the paint and over the paper.

4 When you're happy with the way your painting looks, peel off the tape and leave the paper somewhere to dry.

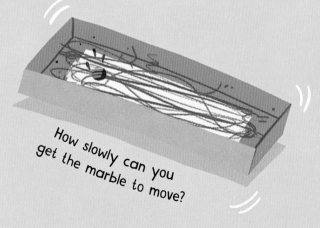

How slowly can you get the marble to move?

5 Now wipe the lid and marble with paper towels before making your next picture. There are several ideas on the opposite page for you to try.

You could see what happens if you start with
DIFFERENT PAINTS...

**...OR
LESS PAINT.**

Use
WHITE PAINT
if you have
black paper.

What do your
pictures look like if
you add two, three
or four marbles to
the lid in step 1?

To keep paint
off parts of your
picture, stick
strips of masking
tape across the
paper before you
drip the paint.

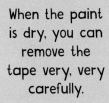

When the paint
is dry, you can
remove the
tape very, very
carefully.

Look at the
striped effect!

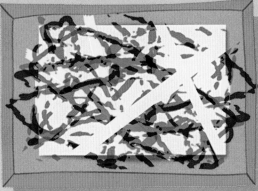

For an extra surprise,
**KEEP YOUR
EYES CLOSED**
until you've stopped
tilting the lid.

After making all your
paintings, remember to wash
the marbles in soapy water.

37

STACKING PYRAMIDS

Make a **BIG** pyramid like the one below from four pyramids that match. You can use the compartments you've created to store different things.

1 Draw a square on a big piece of thick cardboard.

Each side needs to be 20cm (8in) long.

2 Cut out the square. Draw around it twice. Then cut out these squares as well.

3 Place the squares next to each other in a row. Stick masking tape along both joins.

Tape the joins on the other side, too.

4 Place a strip of tape so it overlaps the left edge. Then **FOLD IN** both edges and use the tape to join them together.

5 Now stick one more strip of tape on the outside.

Paint the squares before you tape them together.

6 Make three more pyramids, then stack all four of them, like this.

38

LITTLE BOX ROBOTS

Turn little boxes inside out to hide the designs on them.
Then transform each box into a robot by drawing and sticking on parts.

1 Open all the flaps. Then find where the sides join together and pull them apart carefully.

2 Press the cardboard flat. Crease every fold back on itself.

3 Fold the box back together with the plain cardboard on the outside.

Secure this join with tape.

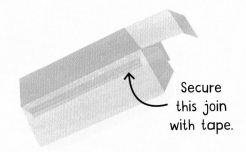

4 Cut out shapes from paper to stick on your robot. Then use a black pen to add more details.

Draw one of these shapes to make a robot arm. Fold this end to glue it on.

Dials

Display screen

Tracks

Buttons

Cogs

39

CARDBOARD SPEECH BUBBLES

Take funny photos and selfies with a giant speech bubble like the ones on this page. Just hold up the speech bubble, next to your face.

1 Glue white paper on top of a big piece of cardboard – or paint it white. Leave it to dry.

2 Use a pencil to draw a speech bubble shape on top. Then paint a thick black line around its edge.

3 Cut out the speech bubble. Now write a message inside with a thick felt-tip pen.

EUREKA!

BOO

AHOY THERE, CAPTAIN

HIP HIP HOORAY

You could use blue paint instead...

...or just cut out your speech bubble without painting the edge.

40

FANTASY MAP

Unfold the largest box you can find to make a very long piece of flat cardboard. Then fill it with drawings and labels to design a map for any place you can imagine.

You could draw a long-lost world...

PYRAMID PASSAGE

...an undiscovered rainforest...

...a city from the future...

TELEPORT STATION

MACHINE KM21

...or an amazing factory.

Keep drawing your map until you've covered every corner and flap.

BIG BUGS

Cut out shapes from cardboard and stick them on in different **LAYERS**, to fill large pieces of paper with 3D portraits of giant bugs.

1 Copy a large version of one of these body shapes onto cardboard.

2 Cut out the shape. Then glue it in the middle of a piece of bright paper.

3 Draw shapes for legs, antennae, wings, eyes and markings onto more cardboard. (Use the ideas on these pages for inspiration.)

4 Cut out all the body parts and stick them onto your picture.

It's easier to paint the cardboard pieces neatly before you stick them down.

Maybe your bug will have
FEARSOME JAWS?

Scrunch up little pieces of foil into shiny eyes.

Stick newspaper on cardboard. Then cut out wing shapes.

This insect can **STING**.

Draw or paint a head, two antennae and six legs like mine directly onto the paper.

Stick **SPOTS** on top of **SPOTS** to create this effect.

Tear corrugated cardboard apart, so you can see its bumpy, rough insides.

43

DANGLING MOBILE

The leaves and flowers in this hanging mobile are made from old egg cartons. You could paint some of the pieces before you thread them together.

1 Draw a heart-shaped leaf inside the lid of an egg carton. Cut it out.

Use a hole punch, or push through a pencil, to make a hole near the top. Then make four more leaves.

x5

2 Now turn the cone-shaped parts from the bases of egg cartons into five flowers...

Pierce a hole at the tip of each cone.

Carefully cut out the cone and snip into its sides.

x5

3 Tie a big knot at the end of three long pieces of string. Thread flowers and leaves onto the strings, following the picture in step 4.

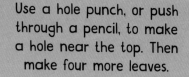

Tie a knot before each flower or leaf you thread on.

4 Tie another long piece of string to each end of a strip of thick cardboard, to make a hanger.

Then tie knots to attach the leaves and flowers to the strip.

CARDBOARD SOLAR SYSTEM

The steps on the next four pages will show you how to turn a large cereal box into a 3D model of the Sun and its eight planets. This is a big project - you don't have to do it all at once.

FIRST, PREPARE THE BOX.

1 Cut off the front of the box. (Keep it to use later.) Then glue these flaps together.

2 Paint the box black. To splatter stars inside, dip a paintbrush in white paint and flick the bristles. Leave it to dry.

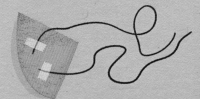

THEN ADD THE SUN.

1 Draw a quarter circle on the piece of cardboard you kept. Place a bowl over one corner and draw around the edge.

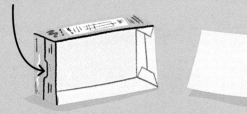

2 Cut out the quarter circle shape.

Save the rest of the cardboard to make the planets.

3 Paint both sides orange. When it's dry, tape two long pieces of dark thread to the back, like this.

4 Hold the Sun in the top left corner of the box. Make pencil marks on the outside to show where the threads should go.

5 Cut a straight slit through each mark. Stop about 3cm (1in) from the back of the box.

6 Guide the threads into the slits. Then pull them tight, to keep the Sun in place.

TURN THE PAGE...

NEXT, MAKE THE PLANETS:

MERCURY
VENUS
EARTH
MARS
JUPITER
SATURN
URANUS
NEPTUNE

START WITH MERCURY...

1 Put the lid of a glue stick on a piece of paper and draw around it. Cut out the circle.

2 Fold the circle in half and half again. Undo the folds.

3 Draw around the circle **TWICE** on the cardboard you used for the Sun. Add dots next to the ends of the folds.

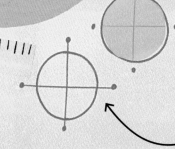

Using a ruler, connect pairs of dots with straight lines, like this.

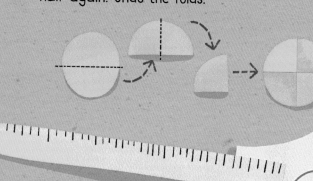

4 Cut out both circles. Then cut into the middle of each circle, along one of the lines only.

5 Paint the circles to look like the picture of Mercury at the top of the page. When they're dry, paint the other sides.

6 Now slot the circles together, like this.

7 Make all the other planets (except for Saturn) in the same way. **BUT** draw around different-sized lids, cups or rolls of tape in step 1, making bigger paper circles for the bigger planets.

Use cardboard from another cereal box if you need more.

...AND FINISH WITH SATURN.

8 Follow steps 1-3, drawing around a cardboard tube instead of the lid because it's a bigger planet. Add a curved line on one side of each circle, about 0.5cm (0.25in) from the edge.

Keep for step 10.

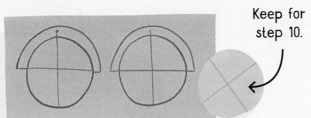

9 Cut out both shapes and cut into the middle from opposite sides, like this.

10 Follow steps 1-3 again, but draw around a mug and draw just **ONE** circle on the cardboard.

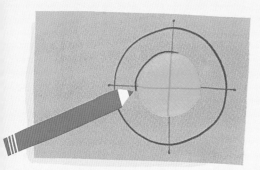

Then put the paper circle from step 8 in the **MIDDLE**, lining up the folds. Draw around it.

11 Cut around the outside edge and then cut the circle out of the middle, following the lines you've drawn.

This leaves a donut shape for Saturn's rings.

12 After painting all three pieces, slot the two matching shapes together. Place the donut shape around them, so it rests on the flat edges that stick out.

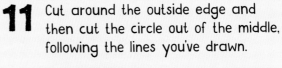

TURN THE PAGE...

NOW HANG THEM IN THE BOX.

1 First, tape a long piece of dark thread to the top of each planet.

2 Next, mark the top of the box in pencil to show where you'll hang each planet. Follow the order of the planets at the top of page 46.

3 Then snip slits into the cardboard and push in all the threads.

You can hide the ends of the threads behind the box.

Pull the planets up or down, so they hang at different heights without touching each other.

Additional design by Carly Davies, Kate Rimmer and Jenny Hilborne
Photographic manipulation by John Russell

Series editor: Jane Chisholm
Series designer: Stephen Moncrieff